Grammar
in practice 1

40 units of
self-study
grammar
exercises

Roger Gower

with tests

CAMBRIDGE
UNIVERSITY PRESS

CAMBRIDGE UNIVERSITY PRESS
Cambridge, New York, Melbourne, Madrid, Cape Town, Singapore, São Paulo

Cambridge University Press
The Edinburgh Building, Cambridge CB2 8RU, UK

www.cambridge.org
Information on this title: www.cambridge.org/9780521665766

First published 2002
4th printing 2007

Printed in Dubai by Oriental Press

A catalogue record for this book is available from the British Library

ISBN 978-0-521-66576-6

Contents

1 a/an

a	*an* (+ vowel sound)
a guitar /g/ 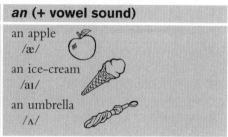	an apple /æ/
a camera /k/	an ice-cream /aɪ/
a uniform /juː/	an umbrella /ʌ/

A Right (✓) or wrong (✗)?

1 **an** office   ✓

2 **an** student   ✗

3 **a** airport

4 **a** station

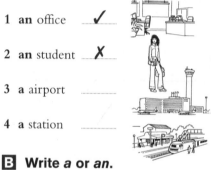

5 **an** university

6 **an** girl

7 **an** engineer

8 **an** aeroplane

B Write *a* or *an*.

1 *a* cup

2 *an* egg

3 _____ telephone

4 _____ envelope

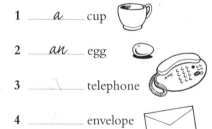

5 _____ newspaper

6 _____ chair

7 _____ orange

8 _____ pen

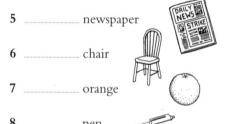

C Write *a* or *an* and the word.

1 *an apple*

2 _____

3 _____

4 _____

5 _____

6 _____

7 _____

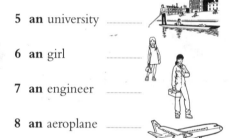

2 radio/radios

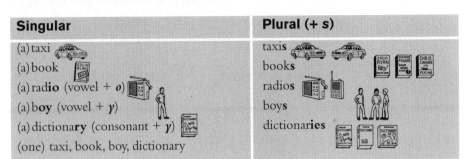

Singular	Plural (+ s)
(a) taxi	taxis
(a) book	books
(a) rad**io** (vowel + *o*)	radios
(a) b**oy** (vowel + *y*)	boys
(a) dictiona**ry** (consonant + *y*)	dictiona**ries**
(one) taxi, book, boy, dictionary	

A Look at the picture. Write the correct words.

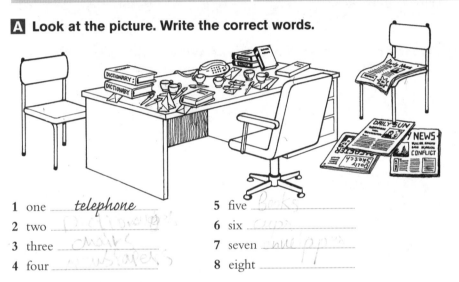

1 one _telephone_
2 two _____
3 three _____
4 four _____
5 five _Books_
6 six _____
7 seven _____
8 eight _____

B Find six words. Make the words plural and write them with the pictures.

T	G	H	U	F
B	K	C	Y	L
V	I	D	E	O
P	B	A	G	W
T	A	B	L	E
Q	B	O	Y	R
X	Y	K	M	Z

1 _flowers_
2 _____
3 _____
4 _____
5 _____
6 _____
7 _____

3 person/people

Singular	Plural	Singular	Plural
(-ch, -sh, -s, -x)	(+ -es)	person	people
(a) wat**ch**	(two) watch**es**	woman	women
dis**h**	dish**es**	man	men
bus	bus**es**	child	children
box	box**es**	foot	feet
(-f/-fe)	(+ -ves)	tooth	teeth
kni**fe**	kni**ves**	tomato	tomatoes
		fish	fish

A Are the plural nouns right (✓) or wrong (✗)?

oranges	1 ✓
6 tomatos	2 ✗
4 apple	3 ✗
onions	4 ✓
6 eggs	5 ✓
2 boxes of matchs	6 ✗
potatoes	7
fishs	8
2 knifes	9
2 dishs	10

B Write plural nouns with the pictures.

glass	fax	dress	shelf
~~brush~~	woman	match	

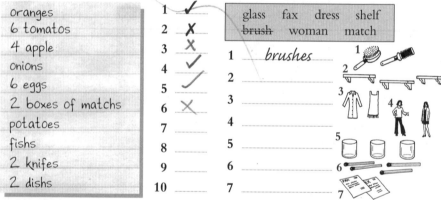

1 _brushes_
2 ....
3 ....
4 ....
5 ....
6 ....
7 ....

C Use the pictures and write plural nouns.

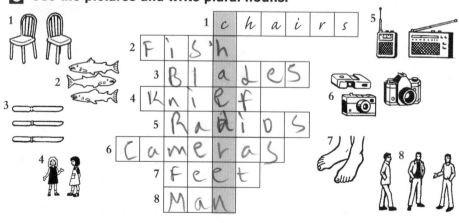

1 c h a i r s
2 F i s h
3 B l a d e s
4 K n i f e
5 R a d i o s
6 C a m e r a s
7 F e e t
8 M a n

4 She's a photographer

Subject	*be*	Singular	Short form
I	am	Tom.	I'm…
You	are	a businesswoman.	You're…
He She Tony	is	a doctor.	He's… She's… Tony's…
It	is	a restaurant.	It's…
		Plural	
We You They Kate and Mary	are	students.	We're… You're… They're… (**not** ~~Kate and Mary're~~)

A Write the subject pronoun.

   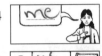

1 *she* 2 *They* 3 *Him* 4 *me*

 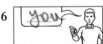  

5 *we* 6 *you* 7 *Her* 8 *us*

B Circle the subject pronoun.

1 (He) / We is an actor.

2 (We) / She are teachers.

3 (She) / They is a doctor.

4 I / (They) are photographers.

5 (She) / I is a businesswoman.

6 We / (He) is a child.

7 (It) / He is a taxi.

8 I / (They) are waitresses.

C Write *am*, *is* or *are*.

1 He ___*is*___ a student.

2 They ___*are*___ doctors.

3 I ___*am*___ a teacher.

4 It ___*is*___ a taxi.

5 You ___*have*___ engineers.

6 We ___*are*___ actors.

7 He ___*is*___ a photographer.

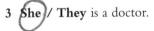
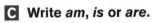

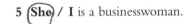

D Write the short form of *be*. Match the sentences with the pictures.

1 They *'re* photographers. [a]

2 She *'s* a doctor. [c]

3 I *'m* a businessman. [E]

4 It *'s* a factory. [b]

5 We *'re* teachers. [D]

a   b

E Read about Mark.

1 He's Mark.

2 He's 23 years old.

3 He's a taxi driver.

First name: Mark   Surname: Ford

Age: 23

Job: Taxi driver

Now write sentences about Sandra, Pete and Anna. Use a subject pronoun and the short form of *be*.

1 *She's* Sandra.

2 *She's 26* years old.

3 *She's* a *doctor*.

4 *They're* Pete and Anna.

5 *are 19* years old.

6 Pete _____ .

7 Anna _____ .

FIRST NAME: Sandra
SURNAME: Lennox
AGE: 26
JOB: Doctor

FIRST NAME: Pete
SURNAME: Young
AGE: 19
JOB: Engineer

FIRST NAME: Anna
SURNAME: Klein
AGE: 19
JOB: Waitress

F Write sentences about you.

I _____ . I _____ years old. I'm a _____ .

5 I'm not from England

Subject	*be*	*not*	Short form
I	am	not	I'm not
he she Simone	is	not	he isn't / he's not she isn't / she's not Simone isn't / Simone's not
it the taxi	is	not	it isn't / it's not the taxi isn't / the taxi's not
we you they Gilbert and George the girls	are	not	we aren't / we're not you aren't / you're not they aren't / they're not Gilbert and George aren't the girls aren't

Jerzy Buzek
Poland

Ryuichi Sakamoto
Japan

Gilbert & George
England

Emmanuel Beart
France

Simone Young
Australia

A Circle the correct form.

1 I **isn't** / (**'m not**) from France.

2 Jerzy Buzek **isn't** / **aren't** from Japan.

3 Susan Saranden and Geena Davis **'m not** / **aren't** from France.

4 Emmanuelle Beart **aren't** / **isn't** from the USA.

5 Ronaldo and Rivaldo **isn't** / **aren't** from Poland.

6 **I'm not** / **isn't** from Canada.

Ronaldo and Rivaldo
Brazil

Susan Sarenden &
Geena Davis USA

B Complete the sentences.

1 Simone Young __isn't__ from Brazil. She__'s__ from Australia.

2 Gilbert and George _____ from Russia. They _____ from England.

3 Ryuichi Sakamoto _____ from England. He _____ from Japan.

4 Susan Saranden and Geena Davis _____ from England. They _____ from the USA.

5 Emmanuelle Beart _____ from Brazil. She _____ from France.

6 I _____ from England. I _____ from _____ .

9

6 There is a computer

there is / there are					Short form
Singular	There	is	a clock.		There's a…
Plural	There	are	two pictures.		

A **Look at the picture. Circle the correct form.**

1 (There's) / There are a mirror.

2 There's / There are two pictures.

3 There's / There are a briefcase.

4 There's / There are a clock.

5 There's / There are three pens.

6 There's / There are a diary.

7 There's / There are an umbrella.

B **Look at the picture. Write *There's* or *There are*.**

1 _____There's_____ a camera.

2 _____ four books.

3 _____ a printer.

4 _____ two phones.

5 _____ three pens.

6 _____ a chair.

7 _____ a computer.

C **Write about your room or office. Use *There's or There are*.**

1 _____ 4 _____

2 _____ 5 _____

3 _____ 6 _____

7 Are you a doctor?

Questions			Positive answer			Negative answer	
Am	I			I	am.		I'm not. / I am not.
Is	he she it	from China?	Yes,	he she it	is.	No,	he she it	isn't. / is not.
Are	you we they			you we they	are.		you we they	aren't. / are not.

A Circle the correct form.

1 (**Are**) / **Is** you from Taiwan?
2 **Am** / (**Is**) she from Malaysia?
3 (**Is**) / **Are** he an engineer?
4 **Am** / **Is** / (**Are**) they teachers?
5 **Is** / (**Are**) you a photographer?
6 **Am** / (**Is**) / **Are** she from Poland?

B Match the questions and the answers.

1 Is the Taj Mahal in China? •   • a No, they aren't.
2 Is Rio de Janeiro in Brazil? •   • b No, she isn't.
3 Is Bill Gates from America? •   • c Yes, he is.
4 Are you a businesswoman? •   • d No, it isn't.
5 Is Venus Williams an engineer? •   • e No, I'm not.
6 Are the Niagara Falls in Japan? •   • f Yes, it is.

C Complete the questions and answers with the correct form of *be*.

1 (_Are_ you from Russia?) (Yes, I _am_ .)
2 (_____ he a doctor?) (Yes, he _____ .)
3 (_____ Jung Chang from New York?) (No, she _____ .)
4 (_____ Tiger Woods and David Duval tennis players?) (No, they _____ .)
5 (_____ you from London?) (No, we _____ .)
6 (_____ the Taj Mahal in India?) (Yes, it _____ .)

8 Is there a bank?

Negative				
Singular	There	isn't	a	station.
Plural	There	aren't	any	buses.

Question				Short answer
Singular	Is	there	a	university?	Yes, there is. No, there isn't.
Plural	Are	there	any	banks?	Yes, there are. No, there aren't.

some/any	
Positive	There are **some** banks.
Negative	There aren't **any** banks.
Question	Are there **any** banks?

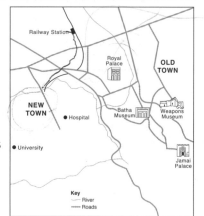

A Look at this map of Fez, Morocco.

Circle the correct form in the sentences about Fez.

1 (There's a) / There are some station.
2 There's a / There are some river.
3 There's a / There are some museums.
4 There's a / There are some university in the new town.
5 There isn't a / There aren't any university in the old town.
6 There isn't a / There aren't any beaches.
7 There's a / There are some palaces.

B Look at the map and answer the questions about Fez.

1 Is there a station? _Yes, there is._
2 Is there a river? _____
3 Are there any museums? _____
4 Are there any beaches? _____
5 Is there a university in the old town? _____
6 Are there any palaces? _____
7 Is there a university in the new town? _____

C Complete the sentences.

In Fez there (1) _are_ museums and there (2) _some_ palaces. There
(3) _aren't_ any beaches but there (4) _is_ a river. There (5) _are_ a
university. There (6) _is_ a station in the old town but there (7) _is_
a station in the new town.

D Look at this map of Vancouver, Canada.

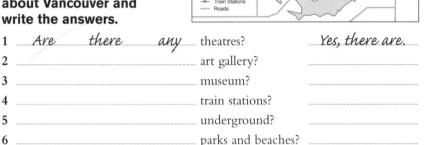

Complete the questions about Vancouver and write the answers.

1 _Are there any_ theatres? _Yes, there are._
2 .... art gallery? ....
3 .... museum? ....
4 .... train stations? ....
5 .... underground? ....
6 .... parks and beaches? ....
7 .... zoos? ....

E Complete the postcard.

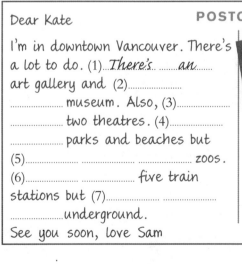

POSTCARD

Dear Kate

I'm in downtown Vancouver. There's
a lot to do. (1) _There's_ _an_
art gallery and (2).....................
.... museum. Also, (3)....................
.... two theatres. (4)....................
.... parks and beaches but
(5).................... .... zoos.
(6).................... .... five train
stations but (7)....................
....................underground.
See you soon, love Sam

9 A new book

<table>
<tr><td>be + adjective</td><td>adjective + noun</td></tr>
<tr><td>It's big.
It isn't small.</td><td>a big pizza
a big, Italian pizza
(not <s>an Italian, big pizza</s>)</td></tr>
</table>

A Circle the correct form.

1 He's (an old man) / a man old.

2 She's a young / (young.)

3 (The watch is **expensive** / an expensive.)

4 They're apples cheap / (cheap apples.)

5 It's a small English dictionary / an English small dictionary.

6 It's big book / (a big book.)

7 The ice-cream is (a cold) / cold.

8 (It's hot coffee) / coffee hot.

9 It's a chair new / (a new chair.)

10 It's old table / (an old table.)

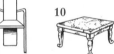

B Complete the signs with an adjective and a noun from the box.

<s>big</s>   cheap   <s>small</s>   English   hot   cold
food   <s>drinks</s>   <s>umbrellas</s>   books   televisions   radios

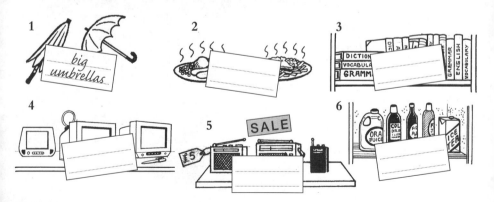

1 *big umbrellas*

10 I've got a car

Positive			Short form	Negative			Short form
He She It	has got		he's got she's got it's got	He She It	has not got		hasn't got
I You We They	have got	a car.	I've got you've got we've got they've got	I You We They	have not got	a car.	haven't got

She's got a new car.

A **Write the sentences with the short form of *have got*.**

1 She has got 6 Swiss Francs. *She's got 6 Swiss Francs.*

2 I have got 60 Indian Rupees. _____

3 We have got 260 Japanese Yen. _____

4 You have got 15 Polish Zloty. _____

5 They have got 3 US Dollars. _____

6 He has got 6 Euros. _____

Who has got the most money? _____

B **Write *hasn't got* or *haven't got*.**

1 (I *haven't got* a coat.)

2 (We _____ an umbrella.)

3 (She _____ a hat.)

4 (He _____ any gloves.)

5 (I _____ a jumper.)

6 (They _____ umbrellas.)

C Complete the sentences about this apartment with *It's got / It hasn't got.*

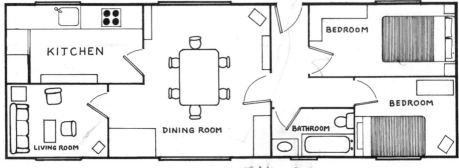

1 *It hasn't got* a garden.
2 *It's hasn't got* a kitchen.
3 *It hasn't got* two bathrooms.

4 *It's got* one bathroom.
5 *It hasn't got* a big living room.
6 *It's got* a big dining room.

D This is Jane and Danny's living room. Complete the sentences with *They've got / They haven't got.*

1 *They've got* a mirror.
2 *They've got* a guitar.
3 *They've got* two armchairs.
4 *They haven't got* any pictures.

5 *They haven't got* a big table.
6 *They've got* a lamp.
7 *They haven't got* a clock.
8 *They've got* a small table.

E Write about you with *'ve got / haven't got.*

1 I *haven't got* a new computer.
2 I *haven't got* an old car.
3 I *haven't got* a guitar.

4 I *'ve got* a video.
5 I *'ve got* a new watch.
6 I *haven't got* two radios.

16

Test 1 (Units 1-10)

A Underline the correct word.

1 **a** / an chair
2 **a** / an office
3 **dictionaries** / dictionarys
4 childs / **children**
5 womans / **women**

[5]

B Write the plural.

1 diary ...... _diaries_
2 potato ...... _potatoes_
3 man ...... _mens_
4 shelf ...... _shelfes_
5 person ...... _persons_

[5]

C Write the short form.

1 I am from Australia. _I'm_
2 She is not from France. _shsb Shen't_
3 There is a shop. _There's_
4 They are not cheap. _They aren't_
5 They have got a car. _They've got_
6 She has not got a diary. _She hasn't got_
7 There are not any pens. _There ain't_
8 It is not noisy. _it ain't_
9 You are not old. _You ain't_
10 I have not got a brush. _I ain't got_

[10]

D Complete the sentences. Use short forms where possible.

– (1) This _is_ Pete. (2) He _'s_ a doctor.
– Hi! (3) _I_ 'm Sandra.
– (4) _where re_ you from Japan?
– No, (5) we _'re_ .
– (6) We _'re_ from China.
– (7) _aren't you_ Pete and Sandra teachers?
– No, (8) _we ain't_ .
– (9) _we ain't_ it expensive?
– Yes, (10) _Later_ .

[10]

E **Write sentences. Use short forms where possible.**

1 There/six people ....

2 There/umbrella ....

3 She/got/apple ....

4 I/not got/clock ....

5 Tom/not got/a computer ....

F **Make the sentences negative.**

1 She's from Poland. ....

2 They're cold. ....

3 The camera's cheap. ....

4 I've got two cars. ....

5 She's got a newspaper. ....

G **Make questions.**

1 you/from Brazil? ....

2 Venus and Serena Williams/tennis players? ....

3 there/any pens? ....

4 there/a university? ....

5 Rio de Janeiro/in Brazil? ....

H **Correct the mistakes.**

1 Are there <u>some</u> oranges? ....

2 There <u>isn't</u> any computers. ....

3 How many hotels <u>is there</u>? ....

4 Is there <u>museum</u>? ....

5 It's <u>expensive car</u>. ....

TOTAL

11 Where's the River Nile?

Question word	Verb	Subject	Short form		
Where	is	the station?	Where's...	Where	
When	is	New Year?	When's...	When	is it?
What	is	your name?	What's...	What	
Who	is	Frieda Kahlo?	Who's...	Who	

A Complete the questions with *where*, *when*, *what*, or *who*. Then write answers for you.

1   _What_'s your name? ....
2   ....'s your job? ....
3   ....'s your birthday? ....
4   .... are you from? ....
5   ....'s the president of your country? ....
6   ....'s your address? ....

B Look at the answers and complete the questions.

1   (_What's_ the Hermitage?)   (It's a museum.)

2   (............ the capital of Bulgaria?)   (Sofia.)

3   (............ Ralph Fiennes?)   (He's an actor.)

4   (............ Chinese New Year?)   (In January and February.)

5   (............ the River Nile?)   (In Africa.)

6   (............ the Rio Carnival?)   (In February.)

7   (............ the Sorbonne?)   (It's a university.)

8   (............ the Andes Mountains?)   (They're in South America.)

9   (............ *The Independent*?)   (It's an English newspaper.)

12 Katherine's brother

	Possessive
Singular one boy a child	**noun + 's** the boy's mother the child's mother
Plural (regular) two boys	**noun + '** the boys' mother
Plural (irregular) two children	**noun + 's** the children's mother

Cherie is Tony Blair's wife. Tony is Cherie's husband. These are Tony and Cherie's children.

! Tony Blair's the British Prime Minister. (=Tony Blair **is**…) He's got four children. (=He **has** got…)

A Complete the sentences. Use possessive forms.

1 Nicholas, Euan and Leo are Tony and ___*Cherie's*___ sons. (Cherie)

2 Katherine is Cherie and _____ daughter. (Tony)

3 Katherine is _____ sister. (Leo)

4 Nicholas is _____ brother. (Katherine)

5 Cherie Blair is Nicholas, Euan, Leo and _____ mother. (Katherine)

6 The _____ father is Tony Blair. (children)

7 Katherine is a _____ name. (girl)

8 The _____ names are Euan, Nicholas and Leo. (boys)

B Look at Cherie's family tree and write about her. Use possessive forms.

1 Her ___*sister's*___ name is Lauren.

2 Her _____ name is Tony Booth.

3 Her _____ name is Gale.

4 Her _____ name is Tony Blair.

5 Her _____ name is Katherine.

6 Her _____ names are Nicholas, Euan and Leo.

7 Her _____ names are Nicholas, Katherine, Euan and Leo.

Tony Booth = Gale

Lauren   **Cherie** = Tony Blair

Nicholas Katherine Euan Leo

13 Have you got the keys?

Questions				Positive answer			Negative answer		
Have	I you we they	got the keys?	Yes,	I you we they	have.	No,	I you we they	haven't.
Has	he she it			he she it	has.		he she it	hasn't.

A Kate and Dan are going on holiday with their children, Karl and Lucy. <u>Underline</u> the correct form.

1 (**Have** / **Has** the children got any sunglasses?)   (Yes, they **have** / **has**.)

2 (**Have** / **Has** you got the keys?)   (No, I **haven't** / **hasn't**.)

3 (**Have** / **Has** he got a suitcase?)   (No, he **haven't** / **hasn't**.)

4 (**Have** / **Has** they got any money?)   (Yes, they **have** / **has**.)

5 (**Have** / **Has** she got a toothbrush?)   (No, she **haven't** / **hasn't**.)

6 (**Have** / **Has** you got the credit card?)   (No, I **haven't** / **hasn't**.)

7 (**Have** / **Has** we got the passports?)   (Yes, we **have** / **has**.)

8 (**Have** / **Has** you got a hat?)   (Yes, I **have** / **has**.)

B Write Kate's questions about Karl and Lucy. Then look at the picture and write Dan's answers.

1 Karl/an umbrella?

Has Karl got an umbrella?　　　　　　　*Yes, he has.*

2 Lucy/a toothbrush?

3 Karl/a passport?

4 they/cameras?

5 Lucy/any books?

6 they/any money?

7 Karl/a radio?

C Answer the questions about you.

1 Have you got a credit card? ....

2 Have you got a British passport? ....

3 Have you got any English money? ....

4 Have you got any English books? ....

5 Has your best friend got a British passport? ....

6 Has your home got three bedrooms? ....

7 Have all your friends got email addresses? ....

14 It's my passport

Subject pronoun	Possessive adjective	
I	my	
you	your	(! you're = you are)
he	his	
she	her	
it	its	(! it's = it is)
we	our	
they	their	(! they're = they are)

Is that **your** suitcase?

No, this is **my** suitcase.

A Complete the sentences with a possessive adjective.

1 This is ....._my_.... passport. (I)

2 They're .... children. (we)

3 They're .... credit cards. (he)

4 It's .... camera. (I)

5 This is .... suitcase. (they)

6 Have you got .... passport? (you)

7 Is this .... radio? (she)

8 What's .... name? (it)

B Circle the correct word.

1 Its / (It's) my umbrella.

2 Have you got **your** / **you're** radio?

3 **Your** / **You're** late!

4 **It's** / **Its** their money.

5 I've got **you're** / **your** passport.

6 It's **they're** / **their** camera.

C Complete the email with possessive adjectives.

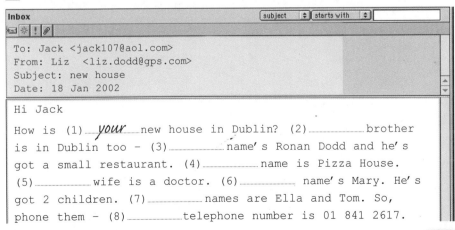

Inbox   subject ⬍ starts with ⬍

To: Jack <jack107@aol.com>
From: Liz <liz.dodd@gps.com>
Subject: new house
Date: 18 Jan 2002

Hi Jack

How is (1) ..._your_... new house in Dublin? (2) .... brother
is in Dublin too – (3) .... name's Ronan Dodd and he's
got a small restaurant. (4) .... name is Pizza House.
(5) .... wife is a doctor. (6) .... name's Mary. He's
got 2 children. (7) .... names are Ella and Tom. So,
phone them – (8) .... telephone number is 01 841 2617.

23

15 I can speak English

	Positive and negative	Question			Answer		
I You He She	can swim.	Can	I you he she	swim?	Yes,	I you he she	can.
It We They	can't swim. (= cannot)		it we they		No,	it we they	can't.

She can speak English.
He can't speak English.

Hello ?

A Look at the job agency questionnaires. Match the people with the jobs in the adverts.

a _____Asha_____   b _____   c _____

a
**Sales people –
Middle East and North Africa**
Can you drive?
Can you speak French and Arabic?

b
Secretary
Can you use a computer?
Can you type 60wpm?

c
Computer Teacher
Can you use a computer?
Can you use the internet?

STAR Job Agency   Agency   Agency

FIRST NAME: Lara   NAME: Asha   NAME: Alain
SURNAME: Clark   ME: Hamid   ME: Pascal

	Lara Clark	Asha Hamid	Alain Pascal
drive	✓	✓	☐
type (60wpm)	☐	☐	✔
use a computer	✓	✓	✔
use the internet	✓	☐	☐
speak French	☐	✓	✔
speak Arabic	☐	✓	☐

B Look at the information in exercise A. Are these sentences true (✓) or false (✗)?

1 Alain can drive. _✗_

2 Lara can use the internet. _____

3 Asha can't type. _____

4 Alain can't speak French. _____

5 Asha can use a computer. _____

6 Lara and Alain can't drive. _____

C Complete the sentences about the three people in exercise A.

1 Lara _can't_ type.

2 Asha _____ drive.

3 Alain _____ speak Arabic.

4 Asha and Alain _____ use the internet.

5 Asha _____ speak French and Arabic.

6 Lara _____ speak French or Arabic.

D Write sentences about you.

1 I _can/can't_ drive.

2 I _____ type.

3 I _____ use a computer.

4 I _____ use the internet.

5 I _____ speak Arabic.

6 I _____ speak English.

E Look at the job adverts and write questions with *can*. Use words from the box.

| drive | speak (French/Arabic) | swim | type | use (the internet) |

1 **FRENCH-SPEAKING SALES PEOPLE** _Can you speak French?_

2 **SWIMMING INSTRUCTOR** _____

3 **ARABIC TEACHER** _____

4 **BUS DRIVERS** _____

5 **INTERNET RESEARCHER** _____

6 **SECRETARY** _____

F Write true answers about you for the questions in exercise E. Use short answers.

1 _____   4 _____

2 _____   5 _____

3 _____   6 _____

16 I'm working

Positive			Short form	Negative			Short form
I	am		I'm	I	am not		I'm not
He			he's	He			he isn't
She	is		she's	She	is not		she isn't
It		reading.	it's	It		working.	it isn't
We			we're	We			we aren't
You	are		you're	You	are not		you aren't
They			they're	They			they aren't

▶▶| Spelling page 63

She isn't working. She's sitting on the train and speaking to a friend on the phone.

A Write the -*ing* form of the verbs.

1 run *running*

2 walk

3 sunbathe

4 lie

5 sit

6 wear

7 write

8 drive

B Look at the picture and complete the sentences with the present continuous.

1 Some boys *are sitting* by the river. (sit)
2 They _____ . (sunbathe)
3 A man _____ on the grass. (lie)
4 He _____ a hat. (wear)
5 A dog _____ near the man. (lie)
6 One boy _____ . (swim)
7 They _____ a good time. (have)
8 The sun _____ . (shine)

C Look at the picture and complete the sentences with the present continuous.

1 The dog *isn't swimming* . (swim)
2 The people _____ . (work)
3 It _____ . (rain)
4 The boy _____ . (drive)
5 The man _____ . (read)
6 The boys _____ coats. (wear)

D Write true sentences about now. Use the present continuous.

1 It/rain today *It isn't raining today.*
2 I/sit in the sun _____
3 I/drive _____
4 I/wear a hat _____
5 I/study English _____
6 I/use a computer _____
7 I/listen to music _____

E Complete the postcard. Use the present continuous.

Dear Mum   POSTCARD

We're in Italy. (1) We *'re staying*
(stay) in a very cheap hotel. It's
great! The sun (2)_____
(shine) and it's very hot so
(3) I _____ (wear) a big
hat. Chris (4)_____
(swim) in the hotel pool and
(5) I _____ (write)
postcards. (6) We _____
(have) a great time.
See you soon
Love Eva

17 a/some

Countable nouns			Uncountable nouns
Singular		**Plural**	cheese
			water
	cup	cups	coffee
a	plate	some plates	some milk
			money
			shampoo
	bottle	bottles	paper
			music

I've got a cup. ✓	I've got three cups. ✓	I've got milk. ✓
~~I've got cup.~~	I've got some cups. ✓	I've got some milk. ✓
~~I've got some cup.~~	I've got two bottles	~~I've got a milk.~~
I've got a bottle	of milk. ✓	~~I've got two milks.~~
of milk. ✓		

A Write *a*, *an*, or *some*.

1 _some_ shampoo   2 _____ bottle   3 _____ money

4 _____ paper   5 _____ box   6 _____ coffee

7 _____ apple   8 _____ apples   9 _____ cheese

B Write *a*, *an* or *some*, and the noun.

1 I've got _some money_ .

2 She's got _a bottle_ of shampoo.

3 I've got _____ of matches.

4 I'm drinking _____ of coffee.

5 There's _____ in the printer.

6 There are _____ .

7 There's _____ on the plate.

8 There's _____ on the radio.

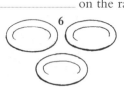

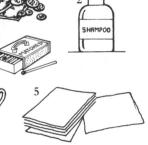

18 Are you working?

Questions			Positive answer			Negative answer		
Am	I			I	am.		I'm not.	
Is	he she it	working?	Yes,	he she it	is.	No,	he she it	isn't.
Are	you we they			you we they	are.		you we they	aren't.

ARE YOU WORKING?

NO, I'M NOT. I'M SITTING ON THE TRAIN.

▶▶ **Spelling page 63**

A Write questions about now. Use the present continuous.

1 the manager/use/a computer? *Is the manager using a computer?*

2 they/have/a meeting in room 1? ....

3 the receptionist/type/a letter? ....

4 the manager/have/lunch? ....

5 it/rain? ....

6 the receptionist/speak/on the phone? ....

7 the sun/shine? ....

8 they/use/computers in room 1? ....

B Look at the picture and write the answers to the questions in A.

1 *No, she isn't.*

2 ....

3 ....

4 ....

5 ....

6 ....

7 ....

8 ....

19 It's mine

Subject pronoun	Possessive adjective	Possessive pronoun
I	my	mine
you	your	yours
he	his	his
she	her	hers
it	its	its
we	our	ours
they	their	theirs

Whose bag is this?
It's mine.

A Complete the sentences with a possessive pronoun.

1 Isabella is a photographer. The camera is ___*hers*___ .

2 Tom is a music teacher. The guitar is _____ .

3 Isabella and Tom have got a new car.
The car keys are _____ .

4 I'm a student. The books are _____ .

5 We are from Spain. The passports are _____ .

6 Have you got a credit card? Is this _____ ?

B Underline the correct form.

1 Is this **your** / **yours** coat?

2 Whose bag is that? It's **their** / **theirs**.

3 Is this my hat or **your** / **yours**?

4 **Her** / **Hers** umbrella's over there.

5 Is this **your** / **yours** jacket?

6 This is **my** / **mine** briefcase.

7 The small umbrella is **our** / **ours**.

LOST PROPERTY

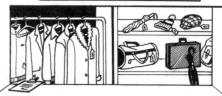

20 Is that a clock?

this (+ singular noun)	**that** (+ singular noun)
This picture is Japanese.	That picture is Japanese.

A Match the pictures and the sentences.

1 (That chair is cheap.) ....*d*.... 5 (Is that table Chinese?) ....

2 (Is this table Chinese?) .... 6 (Is that mirror expensive?) ....

3 (That's an old clock.) .... 7 (This is an old clock.) ....

4 (Is this mirror expensive?) .... 8 (This chair is cheap.) ....

B Complete the sentences with *this* or *that*.

1 ..*That*.. camera's cheap.

2 .... lamp's expensive.

3 .... phone's very small.

4 Is .... TV new?

5 Is .... a Swiss clock?

6 .... is a digital camera.

31

Test 2 (Units 11-20)

A Underline the correct answer.

1 That's **Hillary / Hillary's** car.

2 I've got the **children's / childrens'** passports.

3 It's **they're / their** dog.

4 This is **my / mine** sister.

5 Tom **watching / is watching** TV.

6 Is this his money or **her / hers**?

7 Have you got **cup / a cup** of tea?

8 There's **some / a** water on the table.

9 **This is / That's** the French President on TV.

10 Can you **speak / to speak** French?

| 10 |

B Write the verbs in the present continuous. Use short forms where possible.

1 Tom _____ (not/work).

2 Liz and Karl _____ (swim).

3 We _____ (sunbathe).

4 I _____ (write) a letter.

5 She _____ (not/run).

| 5 |

C Complete the sentences with a possessive form.

1 It's _____ camera. (he)

2 This house is _____ . (we)

3 This isn't _____ car. (his mother)

4 Is the big book _____ ? (they)

5 The small book's _____ . (I)

6 _____ room is there (she).

7 Chelsea is _____ daughter. (Bill and Hillary)

8 He is the two _____ father. (boys)

9 Is this money _____ ? (she)

10 This is the _____ bedroom. (children)

| 10 |

D Write *a, an* or *some*.

1 _____ paper 2 _____ money 3 _____ person

4 _____ people 5 _____ orange

| 5 |

E Look at the answers and write questions.

1 (Mark/his passport?) ....
  'Yes, he has.'
2 (you/your keys?) ....
  'Yes, I have.'
3 (speak/Russian?) ....
  'No, I can't.'
4 (it/rain?) ....
  'Yes, it is.'
5 (Where/Alex and Maria/go?) ....
  'They're going to the bank.'

| 5 |

F Complete the answers.

1 Is she sleeping? Yes, ...
2 Is the sun shining? No, ...
3 Are people swimming? No, ...
4 Can you type? No, ...
5 Have you got a hat? No, ...

| 5 |

G Make the sentences negative.

1 He can drive. ....
2 We're having lunch. ....
3 I'm reading. ....
4 She's studying English. ....
5 They can swim. ....

| 5 |

H Correct the mistakes.

1 Is this <u>you're</u> car? ....
2 Have you got <u>chair</u>? ....
3 He can <u>typing</u> very well. ....
4 <u>What's</u> the president of South Africa? ....
5 <u>She wearing</u> a hat. ....

| 5 |

TOTAL | 50 |

21 Go right

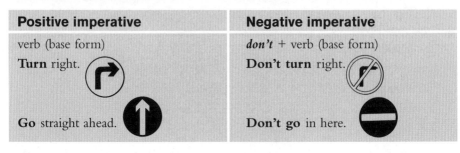

Positive imperative	Negative imperative
verb (base form)	**don't** + verb (base form)
Turn right.	**Don't turn** right.
Go straight ahead.	**Don't go** in here.

A Match the sentences with the pictures.

a   b   c   d   e   f

1 Turn left. _____ *b*

2 Don't take photographs. _____

3 Wash your hands. _____

4 Don't open the window. _____

5 Don't park your car here. _____

6 Be careful! _____

B Complete the sentences with the words in the box.

| open | don't open | ~~wear~~ | don't wear | use | don't use |

1 _____*Wear*_____ a coat. It's raining.

2 Please _____ the window. It's hot in this room.

3 It's OK. _____ my computer. I'm not working on it.

4 _____ a coat. The sun's shining.

5 Please _____ the window. It's cold in this room.

6 Please _____ my computer. I'm working on it.

C Complete the article with an imperative. Use the verbs in the box.

| eat | have | drink |
| ~~sleep~~ | read | |

CAN'T SLEEP?

For a good night's sleep:

1 _____*don't sleep*_____ in a cold bedroom.

2 _____ a hot bath.

3 _____ cheese.

4 _____ warm milk.

5 _____ a book in bed.

22 Them and us

Subject pronouns	Object pronouns	Subject	Verb (+ preposition)	Object
I	me	He	is speaking to	them.
you	you	They	are listening to	him.
he	him			
she	her			
it	it			
we	us			
they	them			

A Underline the correct form.

1 Please take the fax to **she / her**.

2 The manager's here. Alex is talking to **she / her**.

3 I can't see the files. **They / Them** are not here.

4 Can I speak to **he / him**?

5 Write to **we / us**.

6 Can you drive **I / me** to the station?

7 There are two letters on your desk. Please read **they / them**.

B Complete the sentences with a pronoun.

1 Where's my pen? Can you see ___it___?

2 I haven't got the files. Have you got ___?

3 She's at her desk. Go and speak to ___.

4 We can't read this fax. Can you help ___?

5 That's my computer. I'm not using ___.

6 Listen to ___. I've got this great idea!

7 That's ___. He's speaking to the manager.

23 The café is opposite the hotel

My office is **on** the first floor. It's **in** a big building **opposite** the station. It's **next to** a bank.

on	in	next to	opposite

A Complete the questions about the Victoria Hotel with the words in the box.

~~the restaurant~~	the entrance	the reception	the café
the luggage room	room 101	a bathroom	

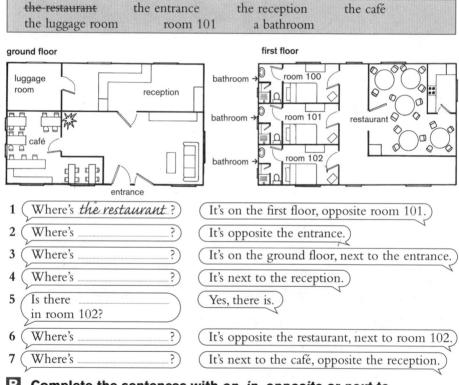

ground floor

luggage room

reception

café

entrance

first floor

bathroom → room 100

bathroom → room 101 · restaurant

bathroom → room 102

1 (Where's *the restaurant*.?) (It's on the first floor, opposite room 101.)

2 (Where's .... ?) (It's opposite the entrance.)

3 (Where's .... ?) (It's on the ground floor, next to the entrance.)

4 (Where's .... ?) (It's next to the reception.)

5 (Is there .... in room 102?) (Yes, there is.)

6 (Where's .... ?) (It's opposite the restaurant, next to room 102.)

7 (Where's .... ?) (It's next to the café, opposite the reception.)

B Complete the sentences with *on*, *in*, *opposite* or *next to*.

Victoria Hotel

Welcome to the Victoria Hotel. The reception is (1) .... *on* .... the ground floor, (2) .... the hotel entrance. The bedrooms are (3) .... the first and second floors. There's a bathroom (4) .... every room. Breakfast is from 7.00 to 10.00 every morning, (5) .... the restaurant. There is also a café (6) .... the ground floor, (7) .... the entrance.

24 She works in London

	Regular verbs					Irregular verbs	
Base form:	work	live	teach	go	study	have	be
he/she/it	works	lives	teaches	goes	studies	has	is

Professor Burke works in London.
She teaches engineering at the
University of West London.

⋙ Spelling page 63

> PROFESSOR FIONA BURKE
> Department of Engineering
> University of West London
> Tel: 01558 985983
> f.burke@wlondon.ac.uk

A Complete the table with a verb in the present simple.

Base form	travel	be	finish	have	get up	manage
he/she/it	1 *travels*	2	3	4	5	6

B Complete the magazine article with the verbs in the box. Use the present simple.

finish	eat	~~be~~	live	go	get up	work

The President's Day

George W Bush (1) __is__ the US President. He (2) _____ with his family in
the White House, in Washington. He (3) _____ for about 11 hours every day.
He (4) _____ at 5:45 am and (5) _____ into his office at 6:45 am. He
(6) _____ a sandwich for lunch and he (7) _____ work at 6 pm.

C Look at the CV. Complete the sentences about Jane with present simple verbs.

Jane Wells
19 Windsor Road
Brighton

mployment
997 to now: Sales Manager (current job)
mpact Books Ltd, London
• manage 3 people
• travel in Europe
• meet customers
• sell books and CD-ROMs

Jane Wells (1) __lives__ in Brighton.
She (2) _____ in London.
She (3) _____ the Sales Manager
for Impact Books. She (4)_____
three people. She (5)_____ in Europe
and (6) _____ customers.
She (7) _____ books and CD-ROMs.

25 These are from Morocco

these (+ plural noun)	**those** (+ plural noun)
These flowers are beautiful.	Those flowers are beautiful.
this (+ singular noun)	**that** (+ singular noun)
This flower is beautiful.	That flower is beautiful.

A Underline the correct form.

1 Is **this** / **these** your book?

2 I work with **that** / **those** woman.

3 **That** / **Those** man's got the keys.

4 **This** / **These** is my sister's child.

5 **This** / **These** children study English.

6 Who are **that** / **those** people?

B The guide is talking about the museum. Look at the picture and complete his sentences with *these, those, this* or *that*.

We've got things from all over the world in (1) ___*this*___ museum. In (2)_____ room we've got work from South America and Africa. The things on (3)_____ table are from Africa. (4)_____ plates are from Morocco and (5)_____ mask is from Kenya. (6)_____ chairs are about 100 years old. (7)_____ three pictures on (8)_____ wall over there are by the Mexican artist, Frieda Kahlo. (9)_____ big picture is by her husband, Diego Rivera. (10)_____ bottles are from Brazil.

26 Coffee comes from Brazil

Positive			Negative		
He She It	works.		He She It	doesn't	work.
Question			**Answer**		
Does	he she it	work?	Yes,	he she it	does.
			No,		doesn't.
Where does	she	work?	In a bank.		

A Write positive or negative sentences. Use the present simple.

1 (coffee/come from Brazil) .... *Coffee comes from Brazil.*
2 (Hillary Clinton/speak Russian) *Hillary Clinton doesn't speak Russian.*
3 (Italy/make pasta)..
4 (the Trans-Siberian railway/go from Moscow to Vladivostok) ....

....
5 (the President of South Africa/live in London) ....

....
6 (the sun/go round the earth) ....
7 (rice/grow in Poland) ....

B Write questions about Sam. Use *does* and the verbs in the box.

speak ~~watch~~ listen drink read wear read drink

1 .... *Does he watch* .... videos?
2 .... to salsa music?
3 .... tea?
4 .... the *Mirror* newspaper?
5 .... coffee?
6 .... French?
7 .... glasses?
8 .... the *Guardian* newspaper?

C Look at the picture of Sam's room and answer the questions in B.

1	*Yes, he does.*	5	
2		6	
3		7	
4		8	

D Write true sentences about a friend.

1 speak/Spanish   *She/He doesn't speak Spanish.*
2 wear/glasses
3 work/in an office
4 come/from Japan
5 live/in Russia
6 go/to football matches
7 speak/English

27 How big is Chile?

Question word	Verb		Answer
How old	are	you?	I'm 30 years old.
How far	is	the station?	It's 10 km.
How big	is	the room?	It's 20 m².
Which train	is	this, the 7 o'clock or the 7.30?	It's the 7.30.
Which keys	are	mine, these ones or those ones?	Those ones.
Why	do	you like Australia?	**Because** it's hot.

A Match the questions and answers.

1 How big is Greenland? •
2 How big is Chile? •
3 Which country is next to Haiti? •
4 How long is the Panama Canal? •
5 How old are the Egyptian pyramids? •
6 Kingston is the capital of which country? •
7 How long is the River Nile? •

• **a** 82 km.
• **b** Jamaica.
• **c** Over 3,500 years old.
• **d** 5,584 km.
• **e** The Dominican Republic.
• **f** 756, 626 km².
• **g** 2,180, 000 km².

B Complete the questions with question words.

a **Old computer for sale (PC)**
(with Wintel software)

b **3 rooms for rent in big house**
1 on ground floor, 2 on first floor
(2 small rooms, 1 big room)

1 (_How big_ is it?) (It's 20 cm x 18 cm.)
2 (.......... is it?) (It's 5 years old.)
3 (.......... room is on the ground floor?) (The big room.)
4 (.......... are you selling it ?) (Because I've got a new computer.)
5 (.......... is it from the town centre?) (It's about 2 km.)
6 (.......... are they?) (22 m², 12 m² and 10 m².)
7 (.......... software has it got, Wintel 98 or Wintel 2000?) (Wintel 2000.)

C Match the questions and the adverts.

1 ... _a_ ... 2 .... 3 .... 4 .... 5 .... 6 .... 7 ....

28 Do you work on Saturdays?

Positive			Negative		
I You We They	work.		I You We They	don't	work.
Question			**Answer**		
Do	I you we they	work?	Yes,	I you	do.
			No,	we they	don't.
Where do	you	work?	In a bank.		

A Read about the college. <u>Underline</u> the 14 present simple verbs.

Welcome to Kingsland College

We <u>have</u> classes in art, music and languages. We have Spanish, Chinese and Arabic this term. All our classes are in the evenings. We don't open in the daytime. Many different people come to Kingsland and a lot of our students have jobs. They work in the daytime, and study at Kingsland College in the evening. Language classes are on Mondays and Wednesdays. They start at 6 pm and finish at 9 pm. Art and music classes are on Tuesdays and Thursdays. They start at 7 pm and finish at 9 pm. We close on Fridays.

B Complete the sentences for students at Kingsland College. Use the positive and negative present simple.

1 (We _don't go_ .... (go) to college in the mornings.)

2 (We .... (go) to college in the evenings.)

3 (I .... (have) a Spanish class on Wednesdays.)

4 (We .... (go) to college on Fridays.)

5 (I .... (learn) Arabic on Tuesdays.)

6 (I .... (learn) Arabic on Mondays and Wednesdays.)

7 (Music classes .... (start) at 6 pm.)

8 (Music classes .... (start) at 7 pm.)

C Answer the questions about Kingsland College. Use short answers.

1 Do classes start at 5 pm? _No, they don't._
2 Do art classes start at 7 pm? _____
3 Do students have classes in the daytime? _____
4 Do students learn Spanish on Tuesdays? _____
5 Do students study music on Thursdays? _____
6 Do Arabic classes finish at 9 pm? _____
7 Do students have classes on Fridays? _____

D Write questions with *you*. Use the present simple.

1 When/go to your music class? (_When do you go to your music class?_

2 study/Chinese (_Do you study Chinese?_

3 When/have a break? (

4 take exams? (

5 Which days/go to college? (

6 What/study? (

7 like your Spanish class? (

8 Why/study in the evenings? (

E Write true sentences for you. Use the present simple.

1 (study Arabic) _I don't study Arabic. / I study Arabic._
2 (eat meat) _____
3 (work in the evenings) _____
4 (study English) _____
5 (live in Japan) _____
6 (drink coffee) _____
7 (wear glasses) _____
8 (play football) _____

29 I usually get the bus

Frequency adverbs

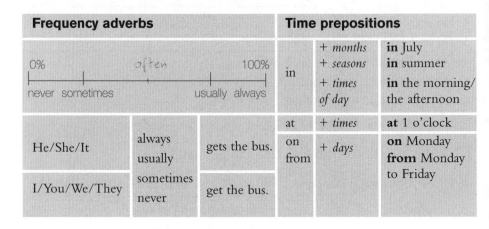

| He/She/It | always usually | gets the bus. |
| I/You/We/They | sometimes never | get the bus. |

Time prepositions

in	+ *months*	**in** July
	+ *seasons*	**in** summer
	+ *times of day*	**in** the morning/ the afternoon
at	+ *times*	**at** 1 o'clock
on from	+ *days*	**on** Monday **from** Monday to Friday

A Look at the survey. Complete the sentences with a frequency adverb and the verb in the present simple.

Transport Survey
How do you get to work?

	7/1	8/1	9/1	10/1	11/1
James Steed	bicycle	bus	bicycle	bicycle	bicycle
Karen Shreck	walk	walk	bus	walk	drive
Andrea Rigg	train	train	train	train	train

1 Karen ___usually walks___ (walk) to work.

2 Andrea _____ (get) the train to work.

3 Karen _____ (drive) to work.

4 James and Andrea _____ (walk) to work.

5 James _____ (cycle) to work.

6 Karen and James _____ (get) the bus to work.

7 Andrea and James _____ (drive) to work.

44

B Write sentences for you. Use a frequency adverb.

1 (get/the bus) *I never get the bus to work.*
2 (drive)
3 (walk)
4 (get/the train)
5 (get/a taxi)
6 (ride/a motorbike)

C Write *in*, *at*, *on* or *from*.

1 *on* Tuesday
2 _____ winter
3 _____ 2 o'clock
4 _____ the morning
5 _____ Thursday
6 _____ Monday to Saturday
7 _____ Friday afternoon
8 _____ August

D Look at the doctors' surgery opening times. Complete the sentences with the present simple and a preposition.

Doctors' surgery opening times*	Monday	Tuesday	Wednesday	Thursday	Friday
10 am – 1 pm	Dr Rooke	closed	Dr Rooke	Dr Rooke	closed
1 pm – 2.30 pm	closed for lunch				
2.30 pm – 4 pm	Dr Snow	Dr Snow	Dr Snow	closed	

*August: surgery closes at 1pm because Dr Snow is on holiday

1 The surgery (open) *doesn't open in* the morning on Tuesdays.
2 Dr Rooke (work) _____ Mondays, Wednesdays and Thursdays.
3 Dr Snow (work) _____ Monday to Wednesday.
4 The surgery usually (open) _____ 10 am.
5 The surgery (close) _____ August for the afternoon.
6 Dr Snow (work) _____ the mornings.
7 The surgery (open) _____ Thursday afternoons.

30 I'd like the menu

like			would like ('d like)	
I/We **like** coffee. (= I/We think coffee is nice.)			I/We**'d like** some coffee. (= I/We want some coffee.)	
Do you **like** tea?	Yes, I **do**.		**Would** you **like** some tea? (= Do you want...?)	Yes, please.
	No, I **don't**.			No, thanks.

A Ask for the things in the pictures with *I'd like / We'd like*. Use the words in the box.

the menu   bottle(s) of mineral water   fish soup
a tomato salad   cup(s) of coffee   the bill

1 (we) _We'd like the menu, please._
2 (I) ....
3 (we) ....
4 (we) ....
5 (I) ....
6 (we) ....

B Underline the correct form.

1 (I like / <u>I'd like</u> some soup.)   (Of course. Fish soup or onion soup?)

2 (**Would you like** / **Do you like** the dessert menu?)   (No, thanks.)

3 (I like / I'd like this restaurant.)   (Me, too. The food is wonderful.)

4 (I'd like / Would you like the bill?)   (Yes, please.)

5 (I like / I'd like a tomato salad.)   (Of course. Large or small?)

6 (**Would you like** / **Do you like** tea with lemon?)   (No, I don't.)

Test 3 (Units 21-30)

A Underline the correct answer.

1 Please **come / to come** here.

2 She's speaking to **we / us**.

3 'Whose bag is it?' 'It's **their / theirs**.'

4 The bank is **next / next to** the hotel.

5 My book is **in / on** the table.

6 Mike **go / goes** to work at 7.00 am.

7 We **doesn't / don't** speak English.

8 Classes start **in / on / at** 9 o'clock.

9 It's always hot **in / on / at** July.

10 Sam **watch / watches** TV every day.

| 10 |

B Write a pronoun.

1 We can't drive. Can you teach .... ?

2 Can you help .... ? I can't do this.

3 Where's the cheese? I can't see ....

4 Jane's got my videos. She likes ....

5 That's my mother. Clare's speaking to ....

| 5 |

C Write the verbs in the correct form.

1 In Russia it .... (snow/always) in winter.

2 Venus and Serena Williams .... (not/live) in Argentina.

3 Jon .... (watch/usually) TV in the evenings.

4 I .... (go/sometimes) to work on Sundays.

5 Ella ....(not/like) tea. She likes coffee.

6 Isabella .... (read/usually) a newspaper on the train.

7 My brother .... (go/never) to college in the mornings.

8 I .... (not/drive) a Volvo.

9 My friends .... (get up/always) at 11.00 am.

10 Sam .... (have/usually) breakfast in the mornings.

| 10 |

D **Complete the questions with *Where, What, How, Why* or *Which*.**

1 '_____ are you?' 'I'm fine, thanks.'

2 '_____ is your bag?' 'It's the red one.'

3 '_____ are you going?' 'To the cinema.'

4 '_____'s your name?' 'Sally.'

5 '_____ are you in bed?' 'Because I'm tired.'

5

E **Write the words in the correct order to make sentences.**

1 do do what you?_____

2 she where does work?_____

3 they when do get up?_____

4 how the Pyramids old are?_____

5 sometimes we the internet use_____

5

F **Complete the questions. Use the words in brackets.**

1 'Where _____ (she/be) now?' 'She's at home.'

2 'What _____ (they/do)?' 'They're engineers.'

3 '_____ (you/like) coffee?' 'Yes, I do.'

4 '_____ (he/work) in the evenings?' 'No, he doesn't.'

5 'When _____ (you/have) breakfast?' 'At 7.30.'

5

G **Correct the mistakes.**

1 They are speaking to <u>he</u>. _____

2 What'<u>s</u> those? _____

3 The café is <u>next</u> the hotel. _____

4 '<u>Do</u> you like some apples?' 'Yes, please.' _____

5 <u>That</u> pictures are beautiful. _____

6 George <u>go</u> to work at 9.30 every day. _____

7 Jane and Mike <u>works</u> in a bank _____

8 Mike always <u>is drive</u> to work. _____

9 Martin <u>he lives</u> in Prague. _____

10 The restaurant's <u>in</u> the ground floor. _____

10

TOTAL **50**

31 I was at a party last night

Positive and negative		Question			Answer		
I	was...		I		Yes,	I	was.
He		Was	he			he	
She	wasn't...		she		No,	she	
It	(= was not)		it	...?		it	wasn't.
We	were...		we		Yes,	we	were.
You	weren't...	Were	you			you	
They	(= were not)		they		No,	they	weren't.
		Where were you?			In the office.		

A **Where were James and Sara on 31 December 1999? Look at their old tickets. Write sentences with the past simple of *be*.**

1 Sara and James ....*were*.... in Glasgow in the evening.

2 Sara .... on a train in the morning.

3 James .... at a football match in the afternoon.

4 They .... at a party in the evening.

5 James .... at the theatre in the afternoon.

6 They .... in London in the evening.

B **Write questions. Use *was* or *were*.**

1 Where/you on 31/12/99? _*Where were you on 31/12/99?*_

2 How old/you in 1999? ....

3 Who/your country's leader in 1999? ....

4 it hot yesterday? ....

5 your friends at your house last weekend? ....

6 Where/you last summer? ....

32 How much oil is there?

	Countable	Uncountable
Positive	There's **a** bottle in the fridge. (singular) There are **some** eggs. (plural)	There's **some** shampoo in the bathroom.
Negative	There aren't **any** tomatoes.	There isn't **any** soap.
Question	How **many** people are there? **A lot.** How **many** taxis are there? **Not many.**	How **much** petrol is there? **A lot.** How **much** oil is there? **Not much.**
Positive	There are **a lot of** people.	There's **a lot of** petrol.
Negative	There are**n't many** taxis.	There is**n't much** oil.

A Complete the table with ✓ or ✗.

	1 *a/an*	2 *some*	3 *any*	4 *much*	5 *many*	6 *a lot (of)*
singular countable noun (*egg*)	✓					
plural countable noun (*eggs*)	✗					
uncountable noun (*oil*)	✗					

B Write C (countable noun) or U (uncountable noun).

1 toothbrush _C_   5 luggage _____

2 toothpaste _____   6 money _____

3 letter _____   7 bread _____

4 paper _____   8 cup _____

C Complete the sentences with *a*, *an*, *some* or *any*.

1 I'd like ___*some*___ tea, please.
2 Is there _____ apple juice?
3 We've got _____ orange juice.
4 Could I have _____ cup of coffee?
5 There's _____ bread on the table.
6 Sorry, there isn't _____ soup.
7 I'd like _____ sandwiches, please.

MENU
Sandwiches
Soup
Orange Juice
Coffee
Tea

D Complete the questions with *How much* or *How many*. Then look at the picture. Write the answers *A lot*, *Not much* or *Not many*.

Bath OIL   SOAP   ASPIRIN   SHAMPOO   Salon 7   SHAMPOO   SHAMPOO   SHAMPOO

1 ___*How much*___ bath oil have we got?   ___*Not much.*___
2 _____ toothpaste have we got?
3 _____ toilet paper is there?
4 _____ aspirins have we got?
5 _____ soap is there?
6 _____ toothbrushes have we got?
7 _____ bottles of shampoo are there?

E Complete the questions with *How much* or *How many*. Then answer the questions about you.

1 ___*How many*___ rooms are there in your house? ___*Five.*___
2 _____ money have you got? _____
3 _____ people are there in your country? _____
4 _____ days do you work every week? _____
5 _____ luggage do you usually take on holiday? _____
6 _____ letters do you write every month? _____

33 He walked on the moon

Past simple

I He She	worked		I finished at 5 pm **last Monday.** I **did**n't go by car **yesterday.**
It We You They	didn't work (= did not)	yesterday.	▶▶ **Spelling page 63.**

A Write the past simple of these verbs in the correct list.

die   drop   ~~invent~~   live   marry   open   paint   play   shop   start   walk

1 +ed	**2** ✗+ied	**3** +d	**4** double consonant +ed
invented			

B Use the verbs in exercise A to make true sentences. Use the past simple.

1 (Marilyn Monroe/Arthur Miller) _Marilyn Monroe married Arthur Miller._

2 (Yehudi Menuhin/guitar) _Yehudi Menuhin didn't play the guitar._

3 (Neil Armstrong/on the moon) ....

4 (The First World War/in 1814) ....

5 (Picasso/Mona Lisa) ....

6 (Alexander Bell/the telephone) ....

7 (Princess Diana/in a car crash) ....

C Write the verbs in the past simple.

Charlotte Brontë was born in 1816 and (1) ...... _lived_ ......
(live) in Yorkshire, England, with her brother and sisters.
They (2) .... (start) to write stories when they
(3) .... (be) children. In 1842, Charlotte went
to Brussels and (4) .... (study) languages.
She also (5) .... (work) as a teacher.

She (6) .... (finish) her novel 'Jane Eyre' in 1847
and it (7) .... (be) very successful. In 1854 she
(8) .... (marry) Arthur Bell Nicholls but they (9) ....
(not have) any children. She (10) .... (die) in 1855.

D Correct the student's essay about Charlotte Brontë.

Charlotte Brontë lived in Ireland. She studied music and she worked
as a teacher in Paris. She finished Jane Eyre in 1842. She married
Constantin Héger in 1854. She died in 1857.

1 _She didn't live in Ireland. She lived in England._
2 ....
3 ....
4 ....
5 ....
6 ....

E Complete the sentences about you.

1 In 1990, ...
2 When I was 10, ...
3 When I was 14, ...
4 Yesterday, I ....
5 Last week, I ....
6 Last January, I ....

34 a/an/the

a/an (+ singular countable noun)	**the**

Can I have **a** bag? (*There are a lot of bags. I want one.*)	Can I have **the** bag? (*He knows which bag.*)
ⓘ *We use* **a/an** *to say what a person/thing is:* My sister is **an** engineer. London is **a** big city.	ⓘ *We use* **the** *when the other person knows which one we mean:* I've got **a** computer and **a** printer. **The** computer is old but **the** printer is new.

A Match the sentences and the pictures.

1 Can I have the bag? _g_ a
2 I'd like an apple. _____
3 I'd like the apple. _____
4 He's painting the door. _____
5 He's painting a door. _____
6 There's a bus. _____
7 There's the bus. _____

B Complete the film review with *a*, *an* or *the*.

Film Review: Cold August

'Cold August' is (1) ___a___ great new film. The story is simple. (2) _____ man and (3) _____ woman are on a week's holiday in Europe. (4) _____ man is (5) _____ writer and (6) _____ woman is (7) _____ artist. They stay for (8) _____ night in (9) _____ small hotel. In (10) _____ morning, (11) _____ man can't find (12) _____ woman anywhere in (13) _____ hotel.

35 I went yesterday

Past simple

Positive	went	had	sat	did
Negative	didn't go	didn't have	didn't sit	didn't do

A Match the past simple forms in the box with the verbs below.

> ate ~~began~~ bought drank drew got up left made
> read said saw spoke taught was/were wrote

1 begin _began_
2 drink _____
3 eat _____
4 draw _____
5 speak _____

6 read _____
7 write _____
8 be _____
9 teach _____
10 say _____

11 leave _____
12 make _____
13 get up _____
14 buy _____
15 see _____

B Complete the sentences. Use some of the verbs in exercise A in the past simple.

Leonardo Da Vinci (1452–1519) (1) _____was_____ an artist, engineer and scientist.
He (2) _____ pictures of plants, animals and people. He also
(3) _____ machines and (4) _____ about them in his notebooks.
He (5) _____ his students about art, science and engineering.
He (6) _____ many languages. He (7) _____ meat because he
(8) _____ a vegetarian.

C What did you do yesterday? Write past simple sentences. Use the verb in brackets.

1 (eat) _I didn't eat a big breakfast yesterday morning._
2 (get up) _____
3 (drink) _____
4 (buy) _____
5 (read) _____
6 (go) _____

36 I'll go tomorrow

Positive			Negative		
I'll/He'll/She'll/We'll/You'll/They'll It will ('ll = will)		go.	I/He/She/It/ We/You/They	won't (= will not)	go.
Question			**Answer**		
Will	I/he/she/it/ we/you/they	go?	Yes,	I/he/she/it/ we/you/they	will.
			No,		won't.

ⓘ *We use **shall I/we** for suggestions*: **Shall I** drive? What **shall we** do?

A Underline the correct form.

1 (What **will you** / **shall you** wear?)

2 (Jack **will** / **won't** be at the party. He's in Japan.)

3 (**It'll** / **It shall** be good fun.)

4 (**Shall we** / **Will we** take some drinks?)

5 (Hurry! **We'll** / **We won't** be late.)

6 (**Will** / **Shall** Anya be there?)

> Come to
> Laura and Ed's Party
> Saturday 8th November
> 8.00 pm
> 15 Hinton Lane

B Complete the message with *will/'ll*, *won't*, or *shall* + verb.

To: s.gold@nrp.com
From: p.smith@nrp.com
Subject: Singapore conference, April 22nd–26th
Date: 4 March 2002

Sara,
Jane (1) _____will be_____ (be) in New York all next month so
(2) she _____ (be) at the Singapore conference. I
think (3) I _____ (get) my plane ticket next
Monday, so (4) _____ I _____ (buy) yours
too? Also, (5) _____ you _____ (see) Jo
next Friday? (6) I _____ (speak) to you tomorrow
morning.
Philip

37 Did you go out yesterday?

Question			Answer		
Did	I/he/she/it/ we/you/they	go?	Yes,	I/he/she/it/ we/you/they	did.
			No,		didn't. (= did not)
When did	she	go?	Yesterday.		

A Read the article about Elvis Presley, then complete the questions.

Elvis Presley made his first rock record in 1953. In 1956 he sang 'Heartbreak Hotel'. It sold millions of records all over the world. In 1957 he went into the US Army. He married Priscilla Beaulieu in 1967. He made 33 films and he sold over 35 million records in total. He died at his home in Graceland in 1977.

1 When ___*did he make his first record*___? In 1953.
2 When _____? In 1956.
3 How many films _____? 33.
4 When _____? In 1957.
5 Who _____? Priscilla Beaulieu.
6 Where _____? At his home in Graceland.

B Answer these questions about you.

1 Where did you live when you were young? _____
2 Did you go out yesterday evening? _____
3 Did you go on holiday last year? _____
4 What did you do last weekend? _____
5 Did it get cold last night? _____
6 Did you phone anyone last night? _____

38 clothes /the clothes

	no article	the
plural and uncountable nouns	Clothes are expensive. (= *all/most clothes*) I like cheese. (= *all/most cheese*)	The clothes in that shop are expensive. I like the cheese in the fridge.
singular countable nouns	ⓘ *Most singular countable nouns have* **the** *or* ***a/an***: a market the market	at home/work (**not** ~~at the home~~) on holiday go to college/work/school have breakfast/lunch/dinner
names	*Most countries*: Brazil, Poland *Towns/cities*: London, Tokyo *Continents*: Africa, Europe *Months*: August, May	*Rivers*: the River Nile *Some countries*: the UK, the USA

A Cross out *the* (t~~h~~e) when we need no article.

A new report by (1) **the** British Government says (2) t~~h~~e people are working (3) **the** long hours. (4) **The** report says 11% of (5) **the** people work over 60 hours every week. Ann Kidd, a lawyer, said (6) '**The** lawyers work long hours, especially in (7) **the** London. I take (8) **the** children to school in (9) **the** morning and then I go to (10) **the** work. I finish at 8.00 in (11) **the** evening. Then I sometimes also work at (12) **the** home.'

B Complete the sentences with *the* or nothing (*X*).

BANGKOK

(1) __X__ Bangkok is the capital of (2)_____
Thailand. It's a great place to go on (3)_____
holiday. You can visit (4)_____ great temple of
Wat Phra Kaew. (5)_____ market in Thonburi
has lots of (6)_____ tourists, but you can buy
(7)_____ cheap clothes there. You will love
(8)_____ food you can buy in Bangkok.

39 When I'm 65

I bought a house **when** I lived in Fez.	**When** I lived in Fez, I bought a house.
I lived in Fez **until** I moved to Paris.	**Until** I moved to Paris, I lived in Fez.
I bought a house **before** I moved to Paris.	**Before** I moved to Paris, I bought a house.

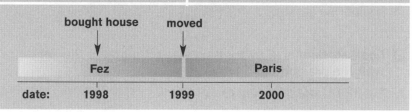

bought house   moved

Fez   Paris

date: 1998   1999   2000

A Circle the correct word.

DRIVING IN THE UK – ADVICE FOR TOURISTS

❶ In the UK you can't drive **when** / (**until**) you are 17 years old.
❷ **Until** / **When** you are in the UK, drive on the left.
❸ Don't use a mobile phone **before** / **when** you are driving.
❹ Don't drive **when** / **before** you are tired.
❺ Plan your journey **before** / **when** you leave.
❻ Don't go **when** / **until** the lights are green.

B Look at the map and complete the directions to the station. Use *when, until* or *before*.

Go along Wood Lane (1) ___*until*___ you see Mill Road. (2)_____ you see Mill Road, turn left. Go along Mill Road (3)_____ you reach the hospital. Turn right into Ash Road (4)_____ you reach the hospital. Turn left (5)_____ you reach the end of Ash Road. Go along Station Road (6)_____ you see the station.

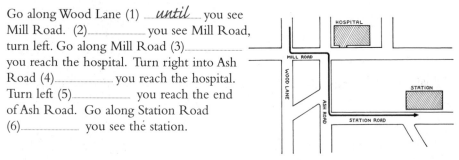

40 I'm working tomorrow

Now	Future
They**'re staying** in London.	They**'re staying** in London **next week**. (= they've got the tickets)

ⓘ *We use the present continuous for future plans (things in a diary):*
I**'m driving** to the airport tomorrow.
When **are** you **having** a party?

A Look at Helen's diary for next week. Complete the sentences with the present continuous.

1 On Monday, *she's driving to Liverpool.*
2 On Tuesday, ...
3 On Wednesday, ...
4 On Thursday, ...
5 On Friday, ...
6 On Saturday, ...

MON drive to Liverpool
TUES have lunch with Katy
WED meet the Sales Managers
THUR fly to Geneva
FRI speak at the IMS conference
SAT stay at the Lake Hotel

B Write questions about Helen's plans. Use the present continuous.

1 you stay/the night in Liverpool (*Are you staying the night in Liverpool?*)
2 When/Katy meet/you? (....)
3 Where/you go/for lunch? (....)
4 the Sales Managers go/to the conference? (....)
5 Which airport/you fly/from? (....)
6 How long/you stay/in Geneva? (....)

C Write sentences about your plans. Use the present continuous.

1 (tonight) *I'm going to the cinema tonight.*
2 (tomorrow) ....
3 (at the weekend) ....
4 (next week) ....
5 (next summer) ....

Test 4 (Units 31-40)

A **Underline** the correct answer.

1 You **aren't / weren't** at work yesterday.
2 The theatre **wasn't / weren't** cheap last night.
3 **How much / How many** people are there?
4 There are **much / a lot of** tomatoes in the fridge.
5 I drink **much / a lot of** coffee every morning.
6 We didn't leave the restaurant **when / until** it closed.
7 Where did you **go / went** yesterday.
8 He **will / shall** be six next year.
9 **When / until** you are in France, drive on the right.
10 'I'm cold.' '**Will / Shall** I close the door?'

$\boxed{10}$

B Complete the sentences with *a, an, some* or *any*.

1 Could I have _____ bread?
2 I haven't got _____ luggage.
3 I'll get _____ plate of cheese.
4 There aren't _____ rooms.
5 I'd like _____ water.

$\boxed{5}$

C Write the verbs in the past simple.

1 stop _____
2 eat _____
3 leave _____
4 go _____
5 have _____
6 do _____
7 shop _____
8 live _____
9 study _____
10 make _____

$\boxed{10}$

D Put the verbs in the correct tense.

1 My sister _____ (go) to America every summer.
2 Ella _____ (see) Mark last week.
3 '_____ (you leave) tomorrow?' 'Yes, I am.'
4 It _____ (not/be) cold next week.
5 We _____ (not/be) at home last night.
6 Asha _____ (be) very tired yesterday.
7 I _____ (go) to the cinema last weekend.
8 Last week he _____ (buy) a computer.
9 We _____ (fly) to Tokyo next week. We've got the tickets.
10 Adrian _____ (not/go) out last night.

| 10 |

E Write questions.

1 '(you/go) _____ to the meeting next Friday?' 'Yes, I am.'
2 Where (you/stay) _____ in London last year?
3 (Shakespeare/live) _____ in London?
4 '(I/make) _____ the tea?' 'Yes, please.'
5 (be/you) _____ in London last week?

| 5 |

F Put *a*, *the* or no article (*X*) in the gaps.

1 I live in _____ Paris. It's _____ big city.
2 I like _____ art. I went to _____ art gallery in Spain last year.
3 Asha goes to _____ work at 8 every morning. She's _____ engineer.
4 'Where are _____ keys?' 'They're on _____ table'.
5 Clare isn't at _____ work. She's on _____ holiday.

| 5 |

G Correct the mistakes.

1 There isn't <u>many</u> paper. _____
2 He <u>not played</u> tennis yesterday. _____
3 She goes <u>to the work</u> at 9 o'clock. _____
4 <u>We meeting</u> the manager next Friday. _____
5 '<u>Have you</u> a party next weekend?' 'Yes, we are.' _____

| 5 |

TOTAL | 50 |

Spelling

Unit 16, 18: verb +*ing*

verb ends in *e*:	*e* +*ing*	verb ends in *ie*:	*i̶e̶* +*y* +*ing*
write	→ writing	lie	→ lying
live	→ living		

verb ends in 1 vowel + 1 consonant:		verb ends in 2 vowels + 1 consonant:	
sw**im**	→ swi**mm**ing	r**ea**d	→ reading
r**un**	→ ru**nn**ing	w**ea**r	→ wearing

Unit 24: verb +*s*/+*es*

verb:	+*s*	verb ends in –*ch*/-*sh*/-*ss*/-*x*/-*o*:	+*es*
work	→ work**s**	tea**ch**	→ teach**es**
start	→ start**s**	fini**sh**	→ finish**es**
live	→ live**s**	g**o**	→ go**es**
get up	→ get**s** up	verb ends in consonant +*y*:	*y̶*+*ies*
manage	→ manage**s**	stu**dy**	→ studi**es**

Unit 33: verb +*ed*

verb +*ed*	finish	→ finish**ed**
verb ends in -*e*: +*d*	like	→ like**d**
verb ends in consonant + *y*: *y̶* +*ied*	car**ry**	→ carri**ed**
one-syllable verb, ends in 1 vowel + 1 consonant:* (*except *w* or *y*)	st**op**	→ sto**pp**ed
	pl**an**	→ pla**nn**ed

ⓘ Vowels: a e i o u
Consonants: b c d f g h j k l m n p q r s t v w x y z

Answer key

Unit 1
A 3 ✗ 4 ✓ 5 ✗ 6 ✗ 7 ✓ 8 ✓
B 3 a 4 an 5 a 6 a 7 an 8 a
C 2 a camera 3 an umbrella
   4 a university 5 a chair 6 an envelope
   7 an ice-cream

Unit 2
A 2 dictionaries 3 chairs 4 newspapers
   5 books 6 cups 7 pens 8 envelopes
B 2 tables 3 boys 4 CDs 5 bags
   6 babies 7 videos

Unit 3
A 3 ✗ 4 ✓ 5 ✓ 6 ✗ 7 ✓ 8 ✗ 9 ✗
   10 ✗
B 2 shelves 3 dresses 4 women
   5 glasses 6 matches 7 faxes
C 2 fish 3 knives 4 girls 5 radios
   6 cameras 7 feet 8 men

Unit 4
A 2 they 3 he 4 I 5 we 6 you 7 she
   8 it
B 2 We 3 She 4 They 5 She 6 He
   7 It 8 They
C 2 are 3 am 4 is 5 are 6 are 7 is
D 2 's (c) 3 'm (e) 4 's (b) 5 're (d)
E 2 She's 26 3 She's ... doctor.
   4 They're 5 They're 19
   6 is an engineer.
   7 is a waitress.
F Answers will vary.

Unit 5
A 2 isn't 3 aren't 4 isn't 5 aren't
   6 'm not
B 2 aren't/'re not ... 're 3 isn't/'s not ... 's
   4 aren't/'re not ... 're 5 isn't/'s not ... 's
   6 'm not ... 'm ...

Unit 6
A 2 There are 3 There's 4 There's
   5 There are 6 There's 7 There's
B 2 There are 3 There's 4 There are
   5 There are 6 There's 7 There's
C Answers will vary.

Unit 7
A 2 Is 3 Is 4 Are 5 Are 6 Is
B 2 f 3 c 4 e 5 b 6 a
C 2 Is ... is 3 Is ... isn't 4 Are ... aren't
   5 Are ... aren't 6 Is ... is

Unit 8
A 2 There's a 3 There are some
   4 There's a 5 There isn't a
   6 There aren't any 7 There are some
B 2 Yes, there is. 3 Yes, there are.
   4 No, there aren't. 5 No, there isn't.
   6 Yes, there are. 7 Yes, there is.
C 2 are 3 aren't 4 is 5 is 6 isn't 7 is
D 2 Is there an ...? Yes, there is.
   3 Is there a ...? Yes, there is.
   4 Are there any ..? Yes, there are.
   5 Is there an ...? No, there isn't.
   6 Are there any ...? Yes, there are.
   7 Are there any ...? No, there aren't.
E 2 there's a 3 there are 4 There are
   5 there aren't any 6 There are
   7 there isn't an

Unit 9
A 2 young 3 expensive 4 cheap apples
   5 a small English dictionary
   6 a big book 7 cold 8 hot coffee
   9 a new chair 10 an old table
B 2 hot food 3 English books
   4 small televisions 5 cheap radios
   6 cold drinks

Unit 10

A 2 I've got 60 Indian Rupees.
  3 We've got 260 Japanese Yen.
  4 You've got 15 Polish Zloty.
  5 They've got 3 US Dollars.
  6 He's got 6 Euros. (He's got the most money)

B 2 haven't got 3 hasn't got 4 hasn't got
  5 haven't got 6 haven't got

C 2 It's got 3 It hasn't got 4 It's got
  5 It hasn't got 6 It's got

D 2 They've got 3 They've got
  4 They haven't got 5 They haven't got
  6 They've got 7 They haven't got
  8 They've got

E Answers will vary.

Test 1 (Units 1 – 10)

A 1 a 2 an 3 dictionaries 4 children
  5 women

B 1 diaries 2 potatoes 3 men 4 shelves
  5 people

C 1 I'm 2 She isn't/She's not 3 There's
  4 They aren't/They're not
  5 They've got 6 She hasn't got
  7 There aren't 8 It isn't/It's not
  9 You aren't/You're not
  10 I haven't got

D 1 is 2 's 3 I 4 Are 5 aren't 6 're
  7 Are 8 they aren't 9 Is 10 it is

E 1 There are six people.
  2 There's an umbrella.
  3 She's got an apple.
  4 I haven't got a clock.
  5 Tom hasn't got a computer.

F 1 She isn't/She's not from Poland.
  2 They aren't/They're not cold.
  3 The camera isn't/The camera's not cheap.
  4 I haven't got two cars.
  5 She hasn't got a newspaper.

G 1 Are you from Brazil?
  2 Are Venus and Serena Williams tennis players?
  3 Are there any pens?
  4 Is there a university?
  5 Is Rio de Janeiro in Brazil?

H 1 any 2 aren't 3 are there
  4 a museum 5 an expensive car

Unit 11

A 2 What 3 When 4 Where 5 Who
  6 What

B 2 What's 3 Who's 4 When's
  5 Where's 6 When's 7 What's
  8 Where are 9 What's

Unit 12

A 2 Tony's 3 Leo's 4 Katherine's
  5 Katherine's 6 children's 7 girl's
  8 boys'

B 2 father's 3 mother's 4 husband's
  5 daughter's 6 sons' 7 children's

Unit 13

A 2 Have ... haven't 3 Has ... hasn't
  4 Have ... have 5 Has ... hasn't
  6 Have ... haven't 7 Have ... have
  8 Have ... have

B 2 Has Lucy got a toothbrush? No, she hasn't.
  3 Has Karl got a passport? Yes, he has.
  4 Have they got cameras? No, they haven't.
  5 Has Lucy got any books? Yes, she has.
  6 Have they got any money? Yes, they have.
  7 Has Karl got a radio? No, he hasn't.

C Answers will vary.

Unit 14

A 2 our 3 his 4 my 5 their 6 your
  7 her 8 its

B 2 your 3 You're 4 It's 5 your 6 their

C 2 My 3 his 4 Its 5 His 6 Her
  7 Their 8 their

Unit 15

A b Alain c Lara

B 2 ✓ 3 ✓ 4 ✗ 5 ✓ 6 ✗

C 2 can 3 can't 4 can't 5 can 6 can't

D Answers will vary.

E 2 Can you swim?
   3 Can you speak Arabic?
   4 Can you drive?
   5 Can you use the internet?
   6 Can you type?

F Answers will vary.

Unit 16

A 2 walking 3 sunbathing 4 lying
   5 sitting 6 wearing 7 writing
   8 driving

B 2 're sunbathing 3 is lying
   4 's wearing 5 is lying 6 is swimming
   7 're having 8 is shining

C 2 aren't working   3 isn't raining
   4 isn't driving 5 isn't reading
   6 aren't wearing

D Answers will vary.

E 2 is shining 3 'm wearing
   4 is swimming 5 'm writing
   6 're having

Unit 17

A 2 a 3 some 4 some 5 a 6 some
   7 an 8 some 9 some

B 3 a box 4 a cup
   5 some paper 6 some plates
   7 some cheese 8 some music

Unit 18

A 2 Are they having a meeting in
      room 1?
   3 Is the receptionist typing a letter?
   4 Is the manager having lunch?
   5 Is it raining?
   6 Is the receptionist speaking on the
      phone?
   7 Is the sun shining?
   8 Are they using computers in
      room 1?

B 2 Yes, they are. 3 No, he isn't.
   4 Yes, she is. 5 No, it isn't. 6 Yes, he is.
   7 Yes, it is. 8 No, they aren't.

Unit 19

A 2 his 3 theirs 4 mine 5 ours 6 yours

B 2 theirs 3 yours 4 Her 5 your 6 my
   7 ours

Unit 20

A 2 a 3 h 4 c 5 g 6 f 7 e 8 b

B 2 This 3 That 4 this 5 that 6 This

Test 2 (Units 11 – 20)

A 1 Hillary's 2 children's 3 their 4 my
   5 is watching 6 hers 7 a cup 8 some
   9 That's 10 speak

B 1 isn't/'s not working 2 are swimming
   3 're sunbathing 4 'm writing
   5 isn't/'s not running

C 1 his 2 ours 3 his mother's 4 theirs
   5 mine 6 Her 7 Bill and Hillary's
   8 boys' 9 hers 10 children's

D 1 some 2 some 3 a 4 some 5 an

E 1 Has Mark got his passport?
   2 Have you got your keys?
   3 Can you speak Russian?
   4 Is it raining?
   5 Where are Alex and Maria going?

F 1 she is 2 it isn't 3 they aren't
   4 I can't 5 I haven't

G 1 He can't drive.
   2 We aren't/We're not having lunch.
   3 I'm not reading.
   4 She isn't/She's not studying English.
   5 They can't swim.

H 1 your 2 a chair 3 type 4 Who's
   5 She's wearing

Unit 21

A 2 a 3 d 4 f 5 c 6 e

B 2 open 3 Use 4 Don't wear
   5 don't open 6 don't use

C 2 have 3 don't eat 4 drink 5 read

Unit 22

A 2 her 3 They 4 him 5 us 6 me
7 them

B 2 them 3 her 4 us 5 it 6 me 7 him

Unit 23

A 2 the reception 3 the café
4 the luggage room 5 a bathroom
6 room 101 7 the entrance

B 2 opposite 3 on 4 in 5 in 6 on
7 next to

Unit 24

A 2 is 3 finishes 4 has 5 gets up
6 manages

B 2 lives 3 works 4 gets up 5 goes
6 eats 7 finishes

C 2 works 3 is 4 manages 5 travels
6 meets 7 sells

Unit 25

A 2 that 3 That 4 This 5 These
6 those

B 2 this 3 this 4 These 5 this 6 These
7 Those 8 that 9 That 10 Those

Unit 26

A 3 Italy makes pasta.
4 The Trans–Siberian railway goes
from Moscow to Vladivostok.
5 The President of South Africa
doesn't live in London.   ·
6 The sun doesn't go round the earth.
7 Rice doesn't grow in Poland.

B 2 Does he listen 3 Does he drink
4 Does he read 5 Does he drink
6 Does he speak 7 Does he wear
8 Does he read

C 2 Yes, he does. 3 No, he doesn't.
4 No, he doesn't. 5 Yes, he does.
6 Yes, he does. 7 No, he doesn't.
8 Yes, he does.

D Answers will vary

Unit 27

A 2 f 3 e 4 a 5 c 6 b 7 d

B 2 How old 3 Which 4 Why
5 How far 6 How big 7 Which

C 2 a 3 b 4 a 5 b 6 b 7 a

Unit 28

A 1 have 2 are 3 don't open 4 come
5 have 6 work 7 study 8 are 9 start
10 finish 11 are 12 start 13 finish
14 close

B 2 go 3 have 4 don't go 5 don't learn
6 learn 7 don't start 8 start

C 2 Yes, they do. 3 No, they don't.
4 No, they don't. 5 Yes, they do.
6 Yes, they do. 7 No, they don't.

D 3 When do you have a break?
4 Do you take exams?
5 Which days do you go to college?
6 What do you study?
7 Do you like your Spanish class?
8 Why do you study in the evenings?

E Answers will vary.
2 I eat meat. / I don't eat meat.
3 I work in the evenings. / I don't
work in the evenings.
4 I study English.
5 I live in Japan. / I don't live in Japan.
6 I drink coffee. / I don't drink coffee.
7 I wear glasses. / I don't wear glasses.
8 I play football. / I don't play
football.

Unit 29

A 2 always gets 3 sometimes drives
4 never walk 5 usually cycles
6 sometimes get 7 never drive

B Answers will vary.

C 2 in 3 at 4 in 5 on 6 from 7 on
8 in

D 2 works on 3 works from
4 opens at 5 closes in
6 doesn't work in 7 doesn't open on

Unit 30

A 2 I'd like fish soup, please.
   3 We'd like two bottles of mineral water, please. 4 We'd like the bill, please.
   5 I'd like a tomato salad, please.
   6 We'd like two cups of coffee, please.
B 2 Would you like 3 I like
   4 Would you like
   5 I'd like 6 Do you like

Test 3 (Units 21 – 30)

A 1 come 2 us 3 theirs 4 next to 5 on
   6 goes 7 don't speak 8 at 9 in
   10 watches
B 1 us 2 me 3 it 4 them 5 her
C 1 always snows 2 don't live
   3 usually watches 4 sometimes go
   5 doesn't like 6 usually reads
   7 never goes 8 don't drive
   9 always get up 10 usually has
D 1 How 2 Which 3 Where 4 What
   5 Why
E 1 What do you do?
   2 Where does she work?
   3 When do they get up?
   4 How old are the Pyramids?
   5 We sometimes use the internet.
F 1 is she 2 do they do 3 Do you like
   4 Does he work 5 do you have
G 1 him 2 are 3 next to 4 Would
   5 Those 6 goes 7 work 8 drives
   9 lives 10 on

Unit 31

A 2 was 3 wasn't 4 were 5 was
   6 weren't
B 2 How old were you in 1999?
   3 Who was your country's leader in 1999?
   4 Was it hot yesterday?
   5 Were your friends at your house last weekend?
   6 Where were you last summer?

Unit 32

A 2 ✗✓✓ 3 ✗✓✓ 4 ✗✗✓ 5 ✗✓✗ 6 ✗✓✓
B 2 U 3 C 4 U 5 U 6 U 7 U
   8 C
C 2 any 3 some 4 a 5 some 6 any
   7 some
D 2 How much … Not much.
   3 How much … Not much.
   4 How many … Not many.
   5 How much … A lot.
   6 How many … A lot.
   7 How many … A lot.
E 2 How much …
   3 How many …
   4 How many …
   5 How much …
   6 How many …
   Answers will vary.

Unit 33

A 1 opened painted played started walked
   2 married
   3 died lived
   4 shopped dropped
B 3 Neil Armstrong walked on the moon.
   4 The First World War didn't start in 1814.
   5 Picasso didn't paint the Mona Lisa.
   6 Alexander Bell invented the telephone.
   7 Princess Diana died in a car crash.
C 2 started 3 were 4 studied 5 worked
   6 finished 7 was 8 married
   9 didn't have 10 died
D 2 She didn't study music. She studied languages.
   3 She didn't work as a teacher in Paris. She worked as a teacher in Brussels.
   4 She didn't finish Jane Eyre in 1842. She finished it in 1847.

5 She didn't marry Constantin Héger.
She married Arthur Bell Nicholls.
6 She didn't die in 1857. She died in
1855.

E Answers will vary.

Unit 34

A 2 e 3 f 4 a 5 b 6 c 7 d

B 2 A 3 a 4 The 5 a 6 the 7 an 8 a
9 a 10 the 11 the 12 the 13 the

Unit 35

A 2 drank 3 ate 4 drew 5 spoke
6 read 7 wrote 8 was/were 9 taught
10 said 11 left 12 made 13 got up
14 bought 15 saw

B 2 drew 3 made 4 wrote 5 taught
6 spoke 7 didn't eat 8 was

C Answers will vary.

Unit 36

A 2 won't 3 It'll 4 Shall we 5 We'll
6 Will 7 Will

B 2 won't be 3 'll get 4 shall ... buy
5 will ... see 6 'll speak

Unit 37

A 2 did he sing 'Heartbreak Hotel'
3 did he make
4 did he go into the army
5 did he marry
6 did he die

B Answers will vary.

Unit 38

A 3 X 4 The 5 X 6 X 7 X 8 the
9 the 10 X 11 the 12 X

B 2 X 3 X 4 the 5 The 6 X 7 X
8 the

Unit 39

A 2 When 3 when 4 when 5 before
6 until

B 2 When 3 until 4 when 5 before
6 until

Unit 40

A 2 she's having lunch with Katy.
3 she's meeting the Sales Managers.
4 she's flying to Geneva.
5 she's speaking at the IMS
conference.
6 she's staying at the Lake Hotel.

B 2 When is Katy meeting you?
3 Where are you going for lunch?
4 Are the Sales Managers going to the
conference?
5 Which airport are you flying from?
6 How long are you staying in
Geneva?

C Answers will vary.

Test 4 (Units 31 –40)

A 1 weren't 2 wasn't 3 How many
4 a lot of 5 a lot of 6 until 7 go
8 will 9 When 10 Shall

B 1 some 2 any 3 a 4 any 5 some

C 1 stopped 2 ate 3 left 4 went 5 had
6 did 7 shopped 8 lived 9 studied
10 made

D 1 goes 2 saw 3 Are you leaving
4 won't be 5 weren't 6 was 7 went
8 bought 9 are flying 10 didn't go

E 1 Are you going 2 did you stay
3 Did Shakespeare live 4 Shall I make
5 Were you

F 1 X ... a 2 X ... an 3 X ... an
4 the ... the 5 X ... X

G 1 much 2 didn't play 3 to work
4 We're meeting 5 Are you having

Acknowledgements

I am very grateful to the following teachers from all around the world who have commented on the material:

Jania Barrell, UK
Vera Dvorakova, Czech Republic
Thérèse Elliott, France
Cinzia Riguzzi, Italy
Peter Strutt, France
Olga Vinogradova, Russia
Lo Wei Yee, Singapore.

I would particularly like to thank Alison Sharpe for her help, guidance and support during the editing of this series. My thanks also to Anna Teevan for her expert editing of the material and to Jo Barker and Tony O'Connell for their excellent design and artwork.

The publisher would like to thank the following for permission to reproduce photographs.
Corbis: pages 8, 9, 11, 13, 26, 27, 52, 53, 57, 58
Associated Press: pages 9, 11, 20
The Photographers Library: page 39
Telegraph Colour Library: page 8